Jewish Wedding Music
Processionals and Recessionals

KOL DODI Vol. II: Instrumental Music
for the Jewish Wedding Service

Arranged by MARY FEINSINGER

BITTERPEARL MUSIC PUBLICATIONS
2350 BROADWAY, SUITE 607
NEW YORK, NY 10024
BITTERPEARL@NYC.RR.COM
WWW.MARYFEINSINGER.COM

©2011

Jewish Wedding Music: Processionals and Recessionals
(KOL DODI **Vol. II: Instrumental Music for the Jewish Wedding Service**)

Full Instrumental Scores and Parts for Various Instruments
and Instrumental Combinations Including
String Quartet, Organ, Trumpet, Flute and Piano

as heard on
KOL DODI: JEWISH MUSIC FOR WEDDINGS 2-CD set
Transcontinental Music–URJ Press No. 95007

Scores for the vocal music on the CDs
are available:
KOL DODI: JEWISH MUSIC FOR WEDDINGS Songbook
Transcontinental Music–URJ Press No. 993107

Copyright ©2011 Mary Feinsinger / Bitterpearl Music Publications
2350 Broadway, Suite 607
New York, NY 10024
U.S.A.
bitterpearl@nyc.rr.com
www. maryfeinsinger.com
ISBN 978–0–615–31436–5

CONTENTS

TRACK
INFORMATION

The music scores in this book may be heard on

KOL DODI: *Jewish Music for Weddings*

(2 CD-set : Transcontinental Music Publications No. 950067)

BOBOVER PROCESSIONAL	CD I, Track 1
KOL SASON RECESSIONAL	CD I, Track 6
GIBRALTAR PROCESSIONAL	CD I, Track 7
MA NA'IM RECESSIONAL	CD I, Track 12
MI VAN SIACH PROCESSIONBAL	CD I, Track 13
MAZL TOV RECESSIONAL	CD I, Track 18
DODI LI PROCESSIONAL	CD I, Track 25
ISRAELI DODI LI	CD II, Track 8
Y'VARECH'CHA	CD I, Track 11

The scores for the vocal music on these CDs are available in
KOL DODI: *Jewish Music for Weddings,* Transcontinental Music Publications No.
993107

www.transcontinentalmusic.com

INTRODUCTION

Two of the most memorable and moving events in a wedding are the processional preceding the marriage ceremony and the recessional that follows. Although it has long been possible to find instrumental music for the celebration *after* a Jewish wedding, there have until now been no collections of instrumental music scores suitable for the Jewish wedding ceremony itself. Couples planning the processional and recessional music for a Jewish wedding have had to settle for secular music, music written for a different religious tradition, or ad hoc arrangements of folk tunes or Israeli popular music.

With this volume, JEWISH WEDDING MUSIC: PROCESSIONALS AND RECESSIONALS, Jewish couples now have fully orchestrated processional and recessional music that is both authentically Jewish and also reflects the solemnity, awe, and joy of the marriage service. The music reflects a variety of Jewish cultures—Eastern European, Sephardic, contemporary American, and Israeli—and has been arranged to provide flexibility in the choice of instruments and instrumental combinations: string quartet, piano solo, organ solo, trumpet, violin or flute with piano, and more.

Some of the music in this book has never before been published. Some are old favorites, newly arranged for inclusion here. Above all, the music in JEWISH WEDDING MUSIC: PROCESSIONALS AND RECESSIONALS is beautiful, reflecting Mary Feinsinger's extraordinary talent, sensitivity, musicality, and deep feeling for Jewish culture. An award-winning composer-arranger and Juilliard graduate, Mary also serves as cantor for the Rossmoor Jewish Congregation and is on the board of directors of the American Society for Jewish music.

While the book stands on its own, it also serves as a companion to KOL DODI (Feinsinger; Transcontinental Publishing), a book of vocal scores for Jewish weddings, and a two CD-set (Feinsinger; Transcontinental Publishing), also called KOL DODI, that contains recordings of pieces in both volumes.

I highly recommend this wonderful collection for cantors and synagogue musicians of all types. It is an invaluable collection and will make choosing processional and recessional music much easier.

Cantor Richard Botton
Cantor Emeritus, Central Synagogue
New York City

Bobover Processional — *Piano Reduction*

[*KOL DODI* CD I, Track 1]

Traditional Wedding March
arr. Mary Feinsinger

Stately March
♩ = 60

BOBOVER PROCESSIONAL — *Piano Reduction*

BOBOVER PROCESSIONAL — *Full Score*
for String Quartet

[*KOL DODI* CD I, Track 1]

Traditional Wedding March
arr. Mary Feinsinger

BOBOVER PROCESSIONAL — *Full Score*

BOBOVER PROCESSIONAL — *Violin I*

Traditional Wedding March
arr. Mary Feinsinger

Stately March
♩ = 60

rit.

BOBOVER PROCESSIONAL — *Violin II*

Traditional Wedding March
arr. Mary Feinsinger

Stately March

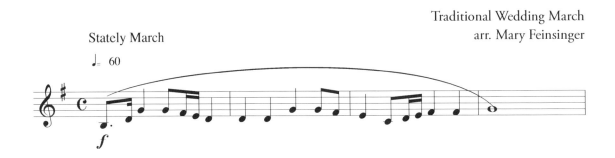

rit.

BOBOVER PROCESSIONAL — *Viola*

Traditional Wedding March
arr. Mary Feinsinger

Stately March
♩ = 60

rit.

BOBOVER PROCESSIONAL — *Violoncello*

Traditional Wedding March
arr. Mary Feinsinger

Stately March
♩= 60

KOL SASON RECESSIONAL — *Piano Reduction*
for String Quartet

[*KOL DODI* CD I, Track 6]

Traditional Wedding Melodies
arr. Mary Feinsinger

KOL SASON RECESSIONAL — *Piano Reduction*

KOL SASON RECESSIONAL — *Full Score*

[*KOL DODI* CD I, Track 6]

Traditional Wedding Melodies
arr. Mary Feinsinger

Con brio ♩= c. 112

KOL SASON RECESSIONAL — *Full Score*

KOL SASON RECESSIONAL — *Violin I*

Traditional Wedding Melodies
arr. Mary Feinsinger

KOL SASON RECESSIONAL — *Violin II*

Traditional Wedding Melodies
arr. Mary Feinsinger

KOL SASON RECESSIONAL — *Viola*

Traditional Wedding Melodies
arr. Mary Feinsinger

Con brio ♩= c. 112

poco rit.   a tempo

KOL SASON RECESSIONAL — *Violoncello*

21

Traditional Wedding Melodies
arr. Mary Feinsinger

GIBRALTAR KOL SASON PROCESSIONAL

for Trumpet in Bb and Piano

[*KOL DODI* CD I, Track 7]

Traditional Sephardic
Wedding Melody from Alan Corré
arr. Mary Feinsinger

GIBRALTAR KOL SASON PROCESSIONAL

23

Kol_____ n'-a - rim_____ mi -mish - te n'-gi - na - tam.]

GIBRALTAR KOL SASON PROCESSIONAL

GIBRALTAR KOL SASON PROCESSIONAL
Trumpet in Bb

Traditional Sephardic
Wedding Melody from Alan Corré
arr. Mary Feinsinger

26

MA NA'IM HECHATAN

RECESSIONAL *for Trumpet in Bb and Piano*

[*KOL DODI* CD I, Track 12]

Melody in Idelsohn,
*Gesänge der
Orientalischen
Sefardim*, 1923
arr. Mary Feinsinger

Ma Na'im Hechatan

Ma Na'im Hechatan — *Trumpet in Bb*

RECESSIONAL
for Trumpet in Bb and Piano

Melody in Idelsohn, *Gesänge der Orientalischen Sefardim*, 1923
arr. Mary Feinsinger

Ma Na'im Hechatan

RECESSIONAL
for Piano Solo

Melody in Idelsohn,
*Gesänge der Orientalischen
Sefardim*, 1923
arr. Mary Feinsinger

Ma Na'im Hechatan

Ma Na'im Hechatan

RECESSIONAL

for Organ Solo

Mary Feinsinger
Melody in Idelsohn, *Gesänge der Orientalischen Sefardim*, 1923
arranged for organ by
Paul Stetsenko

Ma Na'im Hechatan

Mi Van Siach

PROCESSIONAL

for Violin (or Flute) and Piano

[*KOL DODI* CD I, Track 13]

Traditional Melody
arr. Mary Feinsinger

Wedding Liturgy

[MI VAN SI-ACH SHO-SHAN CHO-

CHIM A-HA-VAS KA-LO M'-SOS DO-DIM}

Mi Van Siach Processional

Mi Van Siach Processional

Mi Van Siach Processional

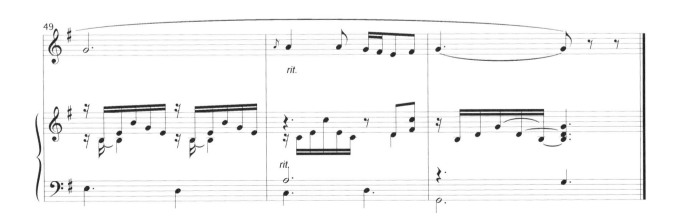

MI VAN SIACH — *Violin (or Flute)*

PROCESSIONAL
for Violin (or Flute) and Piano

Wedding Liturgy

Traditional Melody
arr. Mary Feinsinger

38

001, 2011 BITTERPEARL MUSIC PUBLICATIONS

MAZL TOV RECESSIONAL
for Piano Solo

[*KOL DODI* CD I, Track 18]

Traditional Eastern European
Wedding Melodies
arr. Mary Feinsinger

40

Mazl Tov Recessional

SIMN TOV UN MAZL TOV

Mazl Tov Recessional

41

OD YISHOMA

MAZL TOV RECESSIONAL

Mazl Tov Recessional

DI MIZINKE OYSGEGEBN
(M. Warshawski)

44

Mazl Tov Recessional

DODI LI PROCESSIONAL

for 1 or 2 Flutes (or Violins), Keyboard or Guitar

Steven Sher
arr. Mary Feinsinger

Song of Songs: 2:16, 3:6, 4:9   [*KOL DODI* CD I, Track 25]

Dodi Li Processional

DODI LI PROCESSIONAL

DODI LI PROCESSIONAL

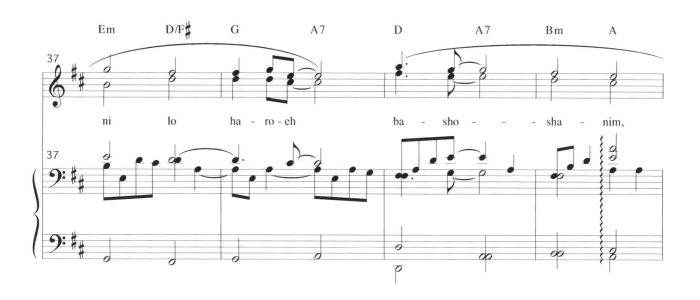

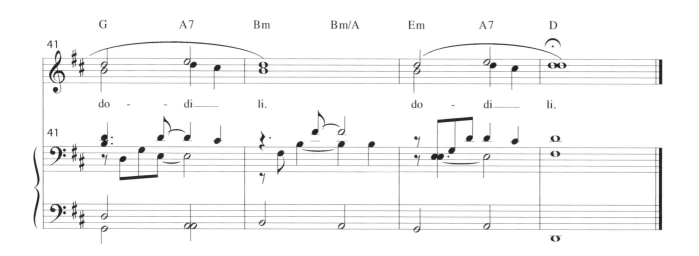

DODI LI PROCESSIONAL — *Flute (or Violin) I and II*

Song of Songs: 2:16, 3:6, 4:9

Steven Sher
arr. Mary Feinsinger

ISRAELI DODI LI

for Flute (or Violin or Oboe or Clarinet in Bb)
and Keyboard

Song of Songs 2:16, 3:6, 4:9

Nira Chen
arr. Mary Feinsinger

[*KOL DODI* CD II, Track 8]

Israeli Dodi Li

mor u-l'vo - na. Do-di li va-a-ni lo ha-ro-e ba-sho-sha-nim. Do-di li va-a-ni lo ha-ro-e ba-sho-sha-nim. Li-bav-ti-ni a-cho-ti ka-la, li-bav-ti-ni ka-la, Li-bav-ti-ni-

Israeli Dodi Li

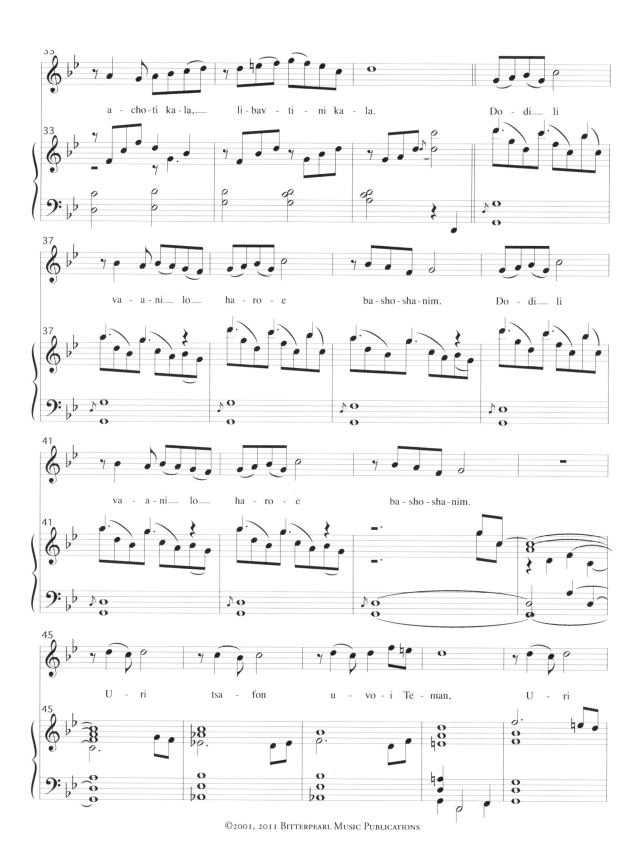

Israeli Dodi Li

ISRAELI DODI LI — *Flute (Violin or Oboe)*

Song of Songs 2:16, 3:6, 4:9

Nira Chen
arr. Mary Feinsinger

54

ISRAELI DODI LI — *Flute (Violin or Oboe)*

ISRAELI DODI LI — *Clarinet in Bb*

Nira Chen
arr. Mary Feinsinger

Song of Songs 2:16, 3:6, 4:9

Israeli Dodi Li — *Clarinet in Bb*

Y'VARECH'CHA

(THREEFOLD BLESSING)

for Two Treble Instruments (Flute, Violin, Oboe),
Keyboard, Optional Violoncello

[*KOL DODI* CD I, Track 1]

Mary Feinsinger
From a Yemenite Melody

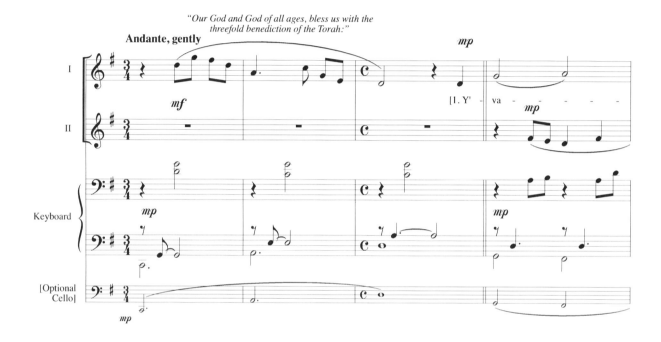

"Our God and God of all ages, bless us with the
threefold benediction of the Torah:"

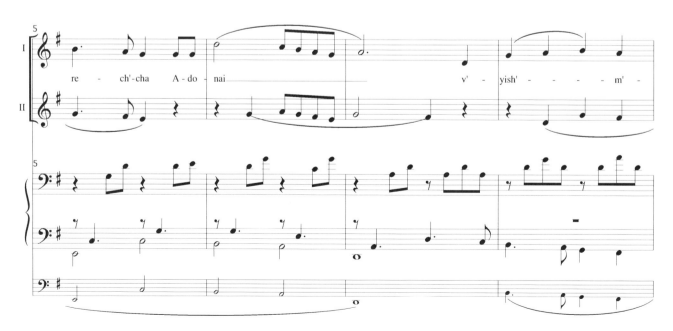

Y'VARECH'CHA

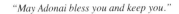

"May Adonai bless you and keep you."

Y'VARECH'CHA

*"May Adonai look kindly upon you
and be gracious to you."*

Y'varech'cha

cha   v' - ya - sem   l' - cha   sha -   lom,_____   sha -

"May Adonai bestow favor on you
and grant you peace."

lom._____   A -   -   -   -   men.]

Y'VARECH'CHA — *Flute (or Violin or Oboe)*
(THREEFOLD BLESSING)

Mary Feinsinger
From a Yemenite Melody

"Our God and God of all ages, bless us with the threefold benediction of the Torah:"

Andante, gently

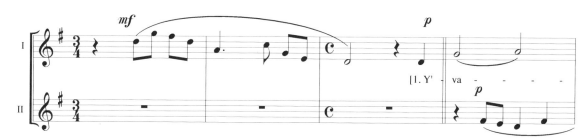

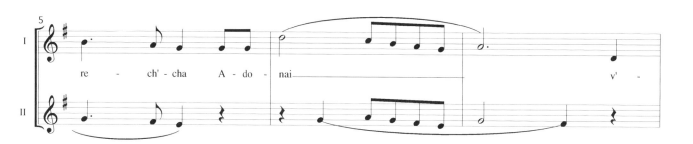

"May Adonai bless you and keep you."

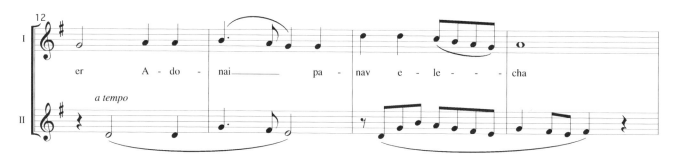

Y'VARECH'CHA — *Flute (or Violin or Oboe)*

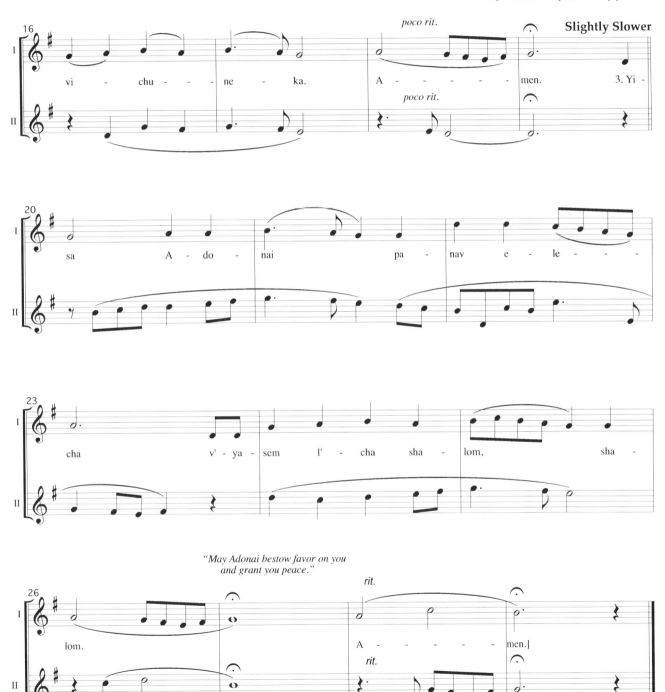

Y'VARECH'CHA — *(Optional) Violoncello*

(THREEFOLD BLESSING)

Mary Feinsinger
From a Yemenite Melody

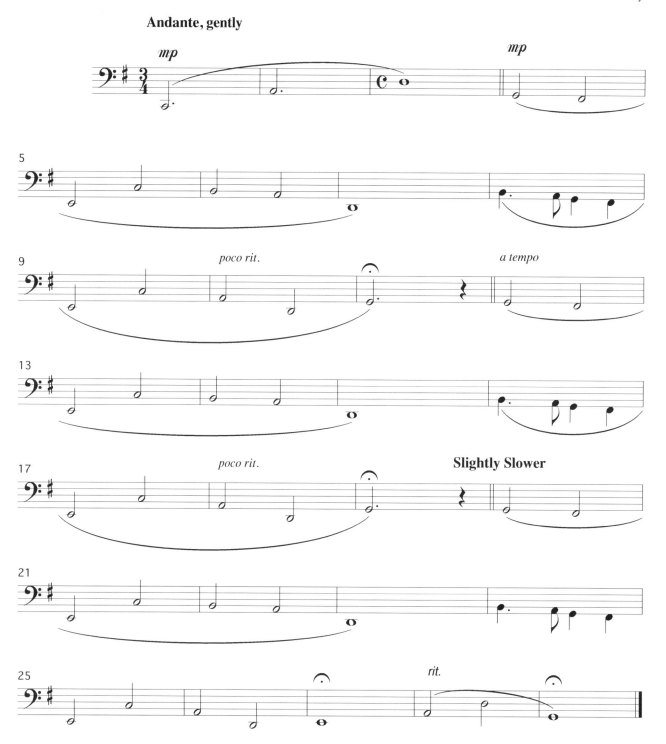